No Nuclear Weapons

The Case for Nuclear Disarmament

Photomontage by Peter Kennard

Text by Ric Sissons

Pluto Press / Campaign for Nuclear Disarmament

August 1945: Japan

'Suddenly a glaring whitish, pinkish light appeared in the sky accompanied by an unnatural tremor which was followed almost immediately by a wave of suffocating heat and a wind which swept away everything in its path. Within a few seconds the thousands of people in the streets in the centre of the town were scorched by a wave of searing heat. Many were killed instantly, others lay writhing on the ground screaming in agony from the intolerable pain of their burns. Everything standing upright in the way of the blast – walls, houses, factories and other buildings – was annihilated . . . Hiroshima had ceased to exist.' – Japanese journalist at Hiroshima.

On 6 and 9 August 1945, over 200,000 people died when the United States dropped two atomic bombs on Hiroshima and Nagasaki. Hundreds of thousands of others were maimed, died prematurely or were born deformed.

Tomorrow: Britain?

After more than 35 years, the threat of nuclear extermination still hangs over the world. What would happen if a one-megaton bomb were to explode 6500 feet over London?

The flash from the explosion would blind people several miles away.

The heat would cause burns 20 miles away.

Most buildings within a radius of 4-5 miles would be demolished. Over half the people in that area would be killed.

Fires would rage over a region with a 10-mile radius.

Later radioactive fallout would cause death or illness through infection and cancer.

Genetic damage would affect the offspring of many survivors.

Communications, energy supply, water services, industry and agriculture would break down.

World War III

In a nuclear war in Europe, at least 100 million people would die.

If the USA and the USSR were engaged in a full-scale nuclear war, at least 200 million would perish.

Spending on arms continues apace. In 1980, world military expenditure totalled $500,000 million or one million dollars every minute. Britain is planning a real, annual 3% growth in defence spending and the United States 4%.

The Other Half

450 million people around the world suffer from malnutrition and hunger. 2,000 million people have no access to dependable sanitary water. 250 million people, in the poorest countries, live in slums or shanty towns.

In Africa only 27% of the population can read and write. There are 455 million jobless or underemployed in the poorer countries and more than 25 million out of work in the richer countries.

Meanwhile world military expenditure is more than double that spent on world health. For the price of two American Trident nuclear submarines, primary schools and teacher training facilities could be provided for half the population of the third world which lacks minimum levels (as per UNESCO standards) of education.

What Is a Cruise Missile?

The Cruise Missile is the most recent addition to the world's nuclear armoury. 20 feet long with a 20-inch diameter it can be launched from land, sea or air. It flies pilotless, under its own power at low altitudes. Its own on-board computer determines a zig-zagging route, making detection difficult. Fired from Britain, a missile could accurately hit a target in Moscow.

Each missile can carry a 200-kiloton warhead 10 times more powerful than the bombs that destroyed Hiroshima and Nagasaki. In comparison to other nuclear weapons the Cruise missile is cheap. The United States intends to deploy 3,000 of the air-launched version.

It is planned that 464 of the ground-launched type will be sited in western Europe, 160 in Britain. At no point have the British people been asked whether they want Cruise missiles.

Who Decided Where to Site the Bases?

Denmark and Norway, although part of the North Atlantic Treaty Organisation – NATO – have refused to allow nuclear weapons on their soil. In 1980 Belgium and Holland deferred the decision as to whether to accept Cruise missiles.

The decision to site Cruise missiles in Britain from 1983 was made at a NATO meeting in Brussels on 12 December 1979. The House of Commons were presented with a *fait accompli* on 24 January 1980. The choice of Greenham Common and Molesworth was announced on 17 June 1980.

There are to be 96 missiles at Greenham Common, near Newbury, Berkshire, and 64 at Molesworth, near Huntingdon. Firing decisions will be taken in Nebraska at United States Air Force Strategic Command. The bases will be staffed by American personnel with British security guards. In the event of war these two bases will be prime targets.

At moments of international tension the missiles will be despatched, in fours, on lorries to their secret firing positions which may be 100 miles from their bases. Regular practice runs will occur every few weeks. The whole area from which the missiles could be fired, from the South coast to the Midlands and across to East Anglia, will be one huge target.

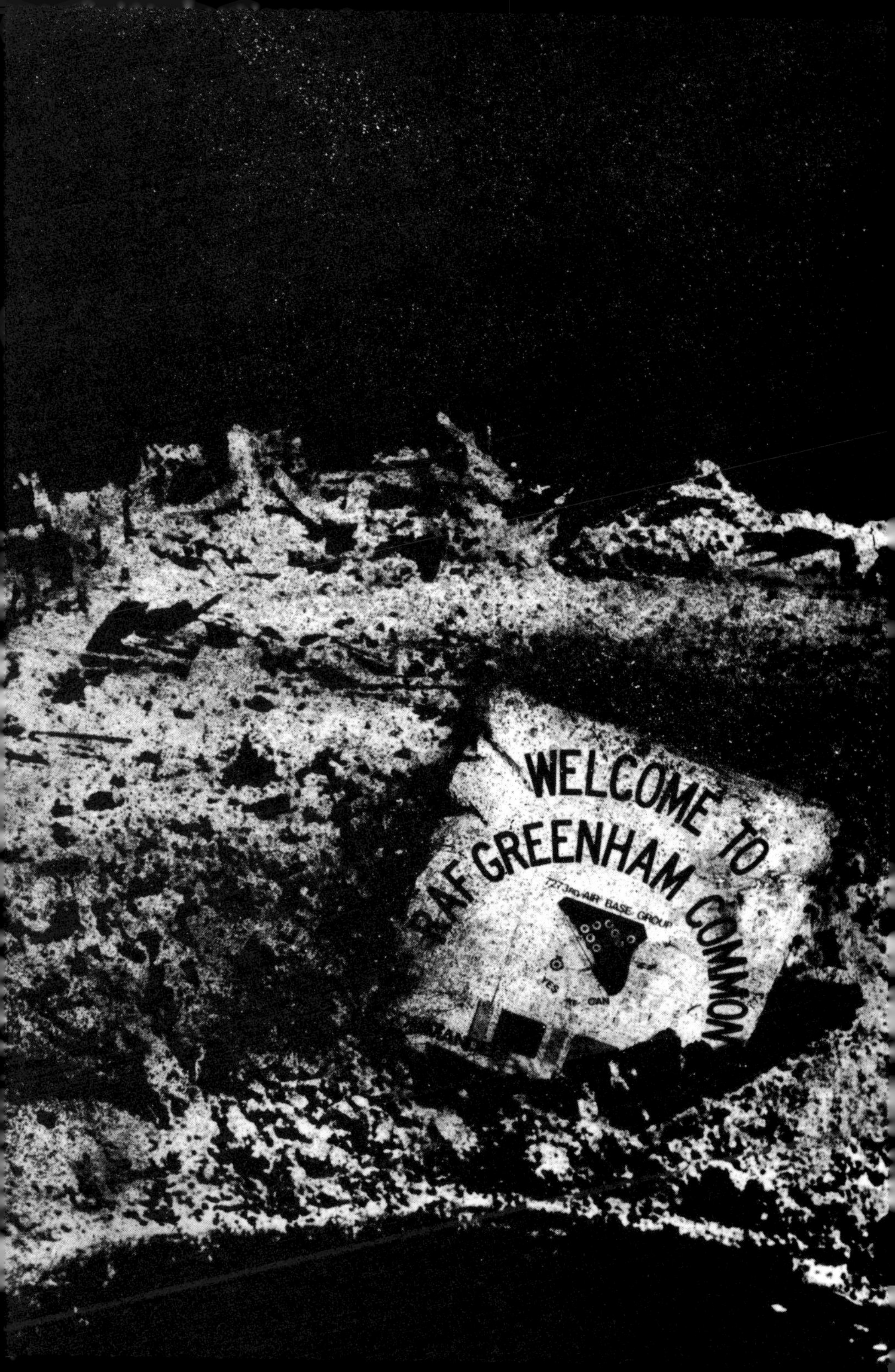
WELCOME TO
RAF GREENHAM COMMON
7273rd AIR BASE GROUP

Polaris

Britain has its own nuclear weapons. The most important is the Polaris submarine. Four are based at Faslane on the Clyde. Each Polaris submarine has 16 missiles which, in turn, have three warheads each.

By today's standards these are old fashioned, but they carry nuclear explosives equal to all the bombs dropped during the second world war. A single missile could devastate any city anywhere on the globe. To do that they would depend on targetting information supplied by American satellites. Although technically possible, it seems very unlikely they would be fired without US consent.

Polaris will be obsolete by 1990. The present Government wants to replace Polaris with four Trident submarines at a cost of well over £5,000 million.

Trident is the most destructive American submarine. Each of its 16 missiles has a range of over 4,500 miles. A single Trident submarine carries 1,000 times more nuclear explosive than was used on Hiroshima and Nagasaki.

THE FIRTH OF CLYDE

A Sense of Priorities

Britain spends more money each year on defence than on health.

The National Health Service is in crisis. Hospitals are being closed. In 1959 there were 548,671 NHS beds; today there are 80,000 less. Queues for treatment are longer, stays in hospital shorter. Community care and preventative medicine are being cut.

Meanwhile Britain maintains a nuclear weapons research programme. The Atomic Weapons Research Establishment at Aldermaston costs £100 million each year to run. That would be sufficient to build four new hospitals, each with 1,000 beds.

Nuclear weapons are produced at Aldermaston and Burghfield. They supply the armaments for the RAF's 207 nuclear-capable aircraft. These are Buccaneers, Jaguars, Nimrods and Vulcans.

The Buccaneers and Vulcans are due to be phased out and replaced by the Tornado Multi-Role Combat Aircraft. 385 are on order, of which 220 will be nuclear-capable bombers.

For the price of the 385 Tornados the Government could build more than 320,000 new homes. That would be more than double the highest annual council house building programme achieved by any Government during the 1970s. In 1979 the local authorities accepted that there were 53,000 homeless households or about 250,000 people.

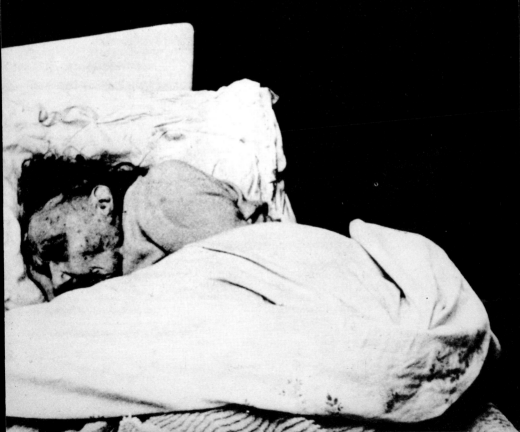

Britain and NATO

NATO is a military and political alliance, established in 1949, covering the Atlantic and western Europe. Britain is one of 15 members. The USA provides and controls most of NATO's nuclear weapons.

NATO accounts for 45% of all world military spending. (SIPRI *Yearbook* 1980)

There are more than 100 American NATO bases in Britain. Trident and Poseidon submarines at Holy Loch on the Clyde, F1-11 bombers at Upper Heyford, Phantom F4 fighter bombers at Alconbury, Bentwaters, Lakenheath and Woodbridge. All carry nuclear weapons.

To back them up there are weapons dumps, stores, communications facilities, transportation terminals, intelligence bases, radar and sonar surveillance. They all receive orders directly from America.

During the abortive attempt to rescue the American hostages in Iran, the East Anglian Lakenheath US air base was on nuclear alert. The British Government was not informed.

In a nuclear war Britain would be a certain target.

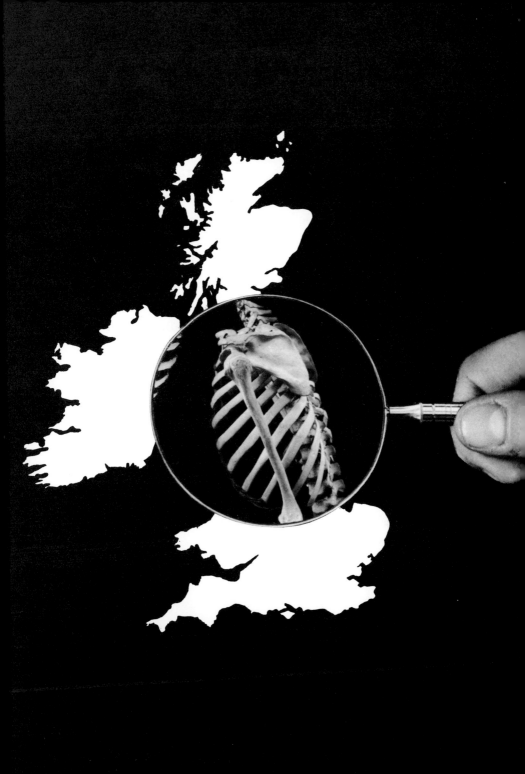

What Price Defence?

'We have to possess the most horrific weapons precisely so as not to use them.'

'I make no secret of the fact that my Ministers and I would like to go more quickly and spend more money.' – Francis Pym, British Defence Secretary, 1980.

Defence is one of the few areas of state expenditure that has not been cut. In the financial year 1979-80, spending rose to £8,558 million. That was 4.6% of gross domestic product.

More money will be required to fulfil promises to the army for new tanks and guns; to the navy for new ships and Trident submarines; and to the air force for the new Tornado nuclear strike aircraft. If these plans are implemented, defence will account for 5.9% of gross domestic product by 1985 and 7.2% by 1990.

Meanwhile:

Inflation is up to 20% a year.

Unemployment is over 2 million.

Health, education and welfare services have been cut by £3,000 million.

Council house building has been stopped.

Labour's Record

Labour Governments share responsibility for the present situation. They have supported Britain's nuclear weapons programme.

In January 1947, the Attlee Labour Government gave the go-ahead for the first British atomic bomb. The decision was taken secretly by a small defence sub-committee. No details were announced. The expenditure was concealed under an item of 'Public Buildings in Great Britain'. There was no discussion in the Labour Party.

When Labour regained office in 1964, it bought Polaris from the USA. This was contrary to the 1961 Party conference decision. The Wilson-Callaghan Government undertook a £1,000 million programme to modernise Polaris. Again, this was a secret decision taken by a small inner group of the cabinet.

Since 1972, Labour Party conferences have voted to support unilateral nuclear disarmament.

Nuclear Weapons around the World

Britain, China, France, India, USA and the USSR have exploded nuclear bombs. Israel and South Africa probably have also made nuclear weapons. Argentina, Brazil, Chile and Pakistan are just four among many who may be members of the nuclear club by the year 2000.

But most nuclear weapons are in the hands of America and the Soviet Union. The USA is estimated to have 9,200 strategic nuclear warheads and the USSR 6,000. These would be used in an all-out war.

In addition there are tactical or theatre nuclear weapons. The USA has 21,000 such warheads and the USSR 15,000. (*World Military and Social Expenditures*, 1980.) Many are located in Europe and include short range missiles and bombs.

The present stockpile of nuclear weapons is far more than is needed to destroy life on earth.

The USA and NATO

'War in our time has become an anachronism. Whatever the case in the past, wars in the future can serve no useful purpose.' – Dwight Eisenhower, former President of the United States.

America's 1981-85 defence plan represents the fastest military growth since 1945 apart from the years of the Korean and Vietnam wars. By 1985, defence expenditure will have doubled. Colossal sums are being spent on more sophisticated nuclear weapons such as the Trident submarine and 3,000 air-launched Cruise missiles for modernised B52 bombers.

The most expensive plans are for the new MX missile system. From 1986, 200 intercontinental ballistic missiles are to be located in 6,000 square miles of Nevada and Utah. That is a land area more than the size of Wales. Each missile has 23 shelters and will be secretly moved from shelter to shelter to avoid detection.

The first will be on alert in 1986 but only after 10,000 miles of road have been laid and 100,000 person-years of labour expended. Costs are rising all the time and will probably exceed $100,000 million.

The USSR and the Warsaw Pact

'We're satisfied to be able to finish off the United States first time round. Once is quite enough. What good does it do to annihilate a country twice? We're not bloodthirsty people.' – Nikita Khrushchev, former Soviet leader.

The Stockholm International Peace Research Institute estimates that in 1979 the USSR's military expenditure totalled $106,000 million. The Soviet Union continues to develop its nuclear capability.

Soviet missiles are probably aimed against all western European countries. One of the latest weapons is the SS 20 Intermediate Range Ballistic Missile. It can carry three independently-targettable nuclear warheads, each with an explosive yield of between 150 and 500 kilotons. It has a range of over 3,000 miles.

The USSR is the lynchpin of the Warsaw Pact. This alliance was established in 1955 after West Germany joined NATO. The Warsaw Pact accounts for 25% of world military expenditure. (SIPRI *Yearbook* 1980)

From Nuclear Energy to Nuclear Weapons

Nuclear power stations make nuclear weapons more widely available. India produced its atomic bombs from the nuclear plants supplied by Canada.

Crude weapons can be made from the nuclear reactor's by-products. Reprocessed plutonium and enriched uranium are used to make nuclear bombs. Recently Brazil purchased a nuclear package from West Germany which included facilities for uranium enrichment and plutonium reprocessing and hence, effectively, for weapons production.

Other dangers exist. Nuclear power stations are a potential health risk to the workers, the local environment and the population at large.

Accidents Will Happen

Nuclear war or devastation could be caused accidentally. The American Government admits that since 1945 there have been 36 serious accidents involving nuclear weapons. Independent estimates put the number at well over 100. (SIPRI *Yearbook* 1977.)

In 1961, a 24-megaton nuclear bomb was jettisoned in North Carolina and nearly exploded. Accidents have also occurred in Europe. One of the most serious was at Palomares, Spain, in January 1966. A mid-air refuelling crash between two American planes led to three 10-megaton nuclear bombs falling on land. One was damaged and caused radioactive contamination. A fourth bomb took several weeks to fish out of the sea.

In the period 1950-76 the US Government admits that there were 16 collisions involving American nuclear submarines in Soviet waters.

While causing immediate damage nuclear accidents can also, mistakenly, convince a Government that they are under attack. Many countries have complex defence systems. These can fail. On average, the US air defence computer gives false nuclear attack alarms twice a week. Four times in the last 18 months these have been taken seriously enough for senior commanders to meet to plan a response.

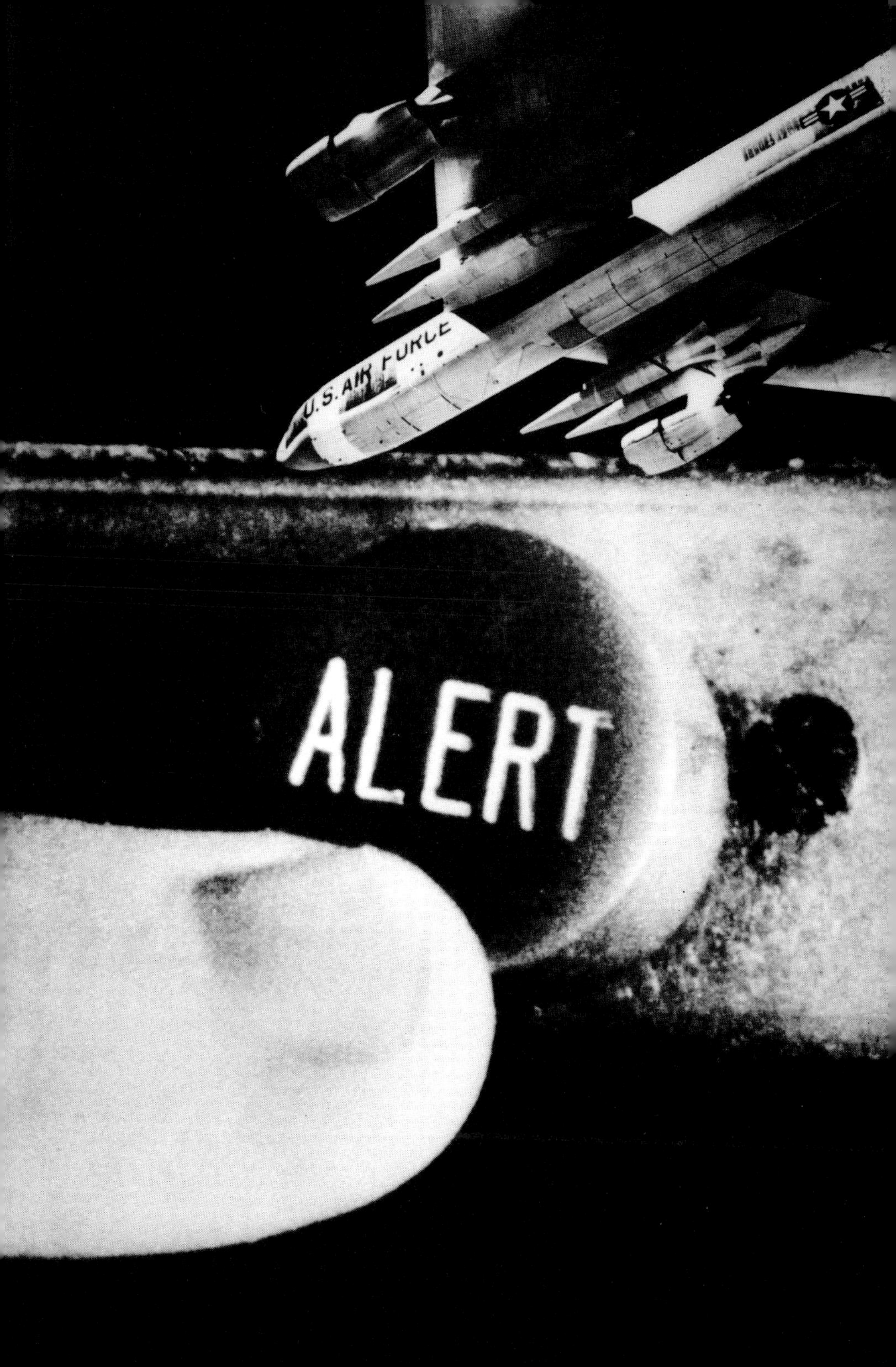
U.S. AIR FORCE
ALERT

Civil Liberties

'It is considered that there is much common ground between war planning and the preparations required for and the organisation appropriate to a major peacetime emergency or natural disaster.' – Home Office Civil Defence Circular ES/1/72.

In times of rising political tension, whether caused by the threat of nuclear war or industrial unrest, extensive plans have been laid for the maintenance of law and order. This could entail the suppression of many civil liberties.

The development of nuclear power and weapons programmes has led to tightening of state security. Installations and the movement of nuclear material are protected by armed guards. Within the plants, the workers undergo security checks and their trade union rights are diminished by security demands. Democracy is threatened by the nuclear state.

If the Bomb Drops

So what do we do if there is a nuclear explosion? The British Government has produced a pamphlet, *Protect and Survive*, giving you advice. When nuclear war threatens, a free copy will be distributed to every household.

Frankly, if you happen to be in the open, at work, in a caravan, living in a bungalow or in the top floors of a block of flats, your chance of survival is poor. But otherwise, using the pamphlet, you can follow three easy steps to make an 'inner refuge'. For fourteen days you will be living under a collection of doors, trunks, sandbags and books. And after that . . .

The Survivors?

For some people the chances of survival are much higher. It is very unlikely that you are one of them. Strengthened underground bunkers are waiting for the Government, local authorities, armed forces and civil service, but not for ordinary people.

A network of tunnels exists beneath the streets of London. Around the country there are regional and sub-regional seats of Government. A national seat of Government also exists, buried deep beneath the countryside, possibly around Bath or Cheltenham.

The Government has plans for the administration of the country in periods of nuclear tension. They include the rounding up of trouble makers, the closure of major roads and, if necessary, the shooting of looters.

The Aftermath

Let us assume that you are not one of the 40 million to die in Britain. You have survived the holocaust. You emerge from your 'inner refuge' after 14 days. What will it be like?

Air Marshall, Sir Leslie Mavor, Principal of the Home Defence College, paints a vivid picture:

'The chances were that those parts of the country holding no nuclear targets would come through more or less undamaged by blast or fire. Their difficulties would be caused by fallout radiation, a large influx of refugees, survival without external supplies of food, energy, raw materials . . . and physical and economic isolation. The main target areas would be so badly knocked about as to be beyond effective self help.'

Coming out of their bunkers the Government will have plenty to keep them busy. Home Office Circular ES8/1976 outlines one of the first jobs:

'When radiological conditions permitted movement, district and borough London controllers should assume that one of the priority tasks for their staff, in the areas where survivors are to continue residing, would be to collect and cremate or inter human remains in mass graves. Once the initial clearance of corpses has been completed, there would still be a problem of several weeks and, perhaps, months, of an above average rate of dying from disease and radiation effects.'

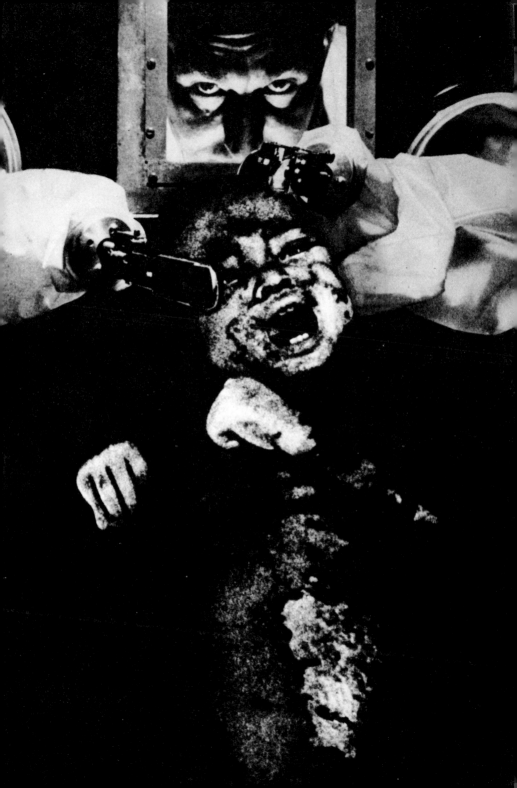

The Real Choice

You do have another option. Campaign against nuclear weapons. Oppose the siting of Cruise missiles in Britain. Demand that the Government cancel Trident, scrap Polaris and all other nuclear weapons. Get Britain out of NATO and close the American bases.

Say No to all Nuclear Weapons.

Whom to Contact

The Campaign for Nuclear Disarmament is actively campaigning against nuclear weapons. They can be contacted at:

11 Goodwin Street, London N4.
Telephone: 01-263 4954.